CORPUS OF MAYA
HIEROGLYPHIC INSCRIPTIONS

VOLUME 2   PART 2   NARANJO
CHUNHUITZ
XUNANTUNICH

CORPUS

OF

MAYA

HIEROGLYPHIC

INSCRIPTIONS

Volume 2   Part 2

IAN GRAHAM

Assistant Curator
of Maya Hieroglyphics
Peabody Museum, Harvard University

PEABODY MUSEUM

OF ARCHÆOLOGY AND ETHNOLOGY
HARVARD UNIVERSITY
CAMBRIDGE, MASSACHUSETTS

1978

ACKNOWLEDGMENTS

Publication of this fascicle was made possible through the generosity of:

Mrs. Katherine Benedict

Mrs. Edmund B. Jackson

Morgan, Grenfell and Company, Ltd. (successors
    to George Peabody and Company)

William F. Parady

Mrs. A. Murray Vaughan

Grateful acknowledgment is made to the Instituto de Antropología e Historia of
Guatemala and to the Office of the Archaeological Commissioner of Belize for their
cooperation in authorizing fieldwork at the sites described in this fascicle. The expenses
of fieldwork were borne by the Stella and Charles Guttman Foundation of New York;
part of the text and illustrations were prepared during the period of a three-year
grant from the National Endowment for the Humanities.

Naranjo, Stela 25

LOCATION   Northernmost of the rear row of stelae set on the terrace in front of Structure C-9. The stela was removed to Flores in 1971.

CONDITION   Broken into two halves, with a piece missing at the break. The lower half was still standing when Maler found it. Most of the sculptured surface is quite well preserved.

MATERIAL   A hard limestone.

SHAPE   Parallel sides, with rounded top.

DIMENSIONS

HLC	1.86 m	
PB	0.80 m	
MW	0.70 m	
WBC	0.67 m	
MTh	0.31 m	
Rel	1.2 cm	

CARVED AREAS   Front carved in relief; both sides carry incised inscriptions.

PHOTOGRAPHS   Morley, 1921.

DRAWINGS   Front: von Euw, based on field drawings corrected by artificial light. Sides: Graham, based on field drawings and a photograph of the upper right-hand side with the glyphs inked in.

REMARKS   At B8, a third numerical dot can be faintly distinguished, although a month position number of three cannot properly occur with the day Kan. At C10, the position number in the month Zip is very clearly 18, whereas 17 is called for.

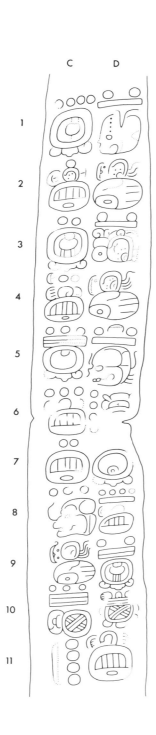

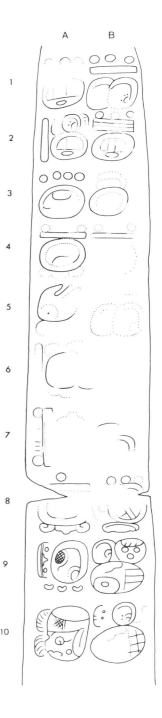

Left side

Right side

Naranjo, Stela 26

LOCATION   Stated by Maler to have been the central member of a line of three stelae at the rear on the terrace in front of Structure C-9.

CONDITION   Broken into fragments of which Morley found two. In 1970 only one could be found, the same one that Morley illustrated.

MATERIAL   A schistose stone of grayish brown color.

SHAPE   Unknown.

DIMENSIONS

HLC	0.33 m plus
PB	0.62 m
MW	0.84 m
WBC	unknown
MTh	0.25 m plus
Rel	2.0 cm

CARVED AREAS   Unknown.

PHOTOGRAPH   Morley, 1922.

DRAWING   Graham, based on field drawing corrrected by artificial light.

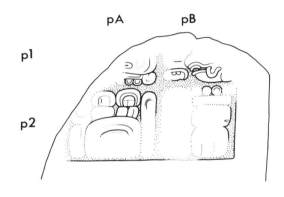

Naranjo, Stela 27

LOCATION Southernmost of the rear row of stelae set on the terrace in front of Structure C-9. Removed to Melchor de Mencos in 1972.

CONDITION Broken into several pieces of which Morley found three, one of them smooth on both faces and therefore presumably part of the butt. In 1971 another sculptured fragment was found and is illustrated here.

MATERIAL Fine-grained limestone. Maler's poor opinion of its quality may have been due to belief that a once-existing high relief had rather rapidly been reduced by action of the weather.

SHAPE Unknown.

DIMENSIONS HLC 0.73 m plus
PB 0.47 m
MW 0.67 m plus
WBC unknown
MTh 0.30 m
Rel 0.9 cm

CARVED AREAS Front only.

PHOTOGRAPH Graham, 1971.

DRAWING Graham, based on a field drawing corrected by artificial light.

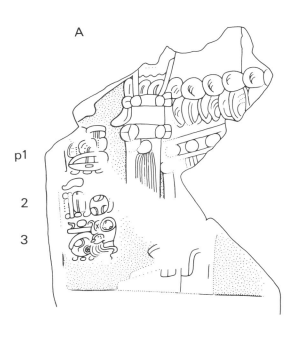

Naranjo, Stela 28

LOCATION Northernmost in the front row of four stelae on the terrace in front of Structure C-9. Removed to Flores in 1972.

CONDITION Maler found the stela broken into three pieces, with most of the butt also broken off in the ground. The front had suffered considerable erosion, the back much more. Over the next half century the back lost more of its relief, and became more deeply pitted.

MATERIAL Limestone.

SHAPE Almost parallel sides, with flattish top.

DIMENSIONS
HLC	2.34 m	
PB	0.27 m plus	
MW	1.25 m	
WBC	1.20 m approx.	
MTh	0.46 m	
Rel	4.0 cm	

CARVED AREAS Front and back.

PHOTOGRAPHS Front: reproduced from Maler's original negatives of 1905. Back: Morley, 1921. Stereophotos: Graham, 1972.

DRAWINGS Front: von Euw, based on field drawings corrected by artificial light. Back: Graham, based mainly on Morley's photographs and to a lesser extent, because the surface has deteriorated, on stereophotos and a field drawing.

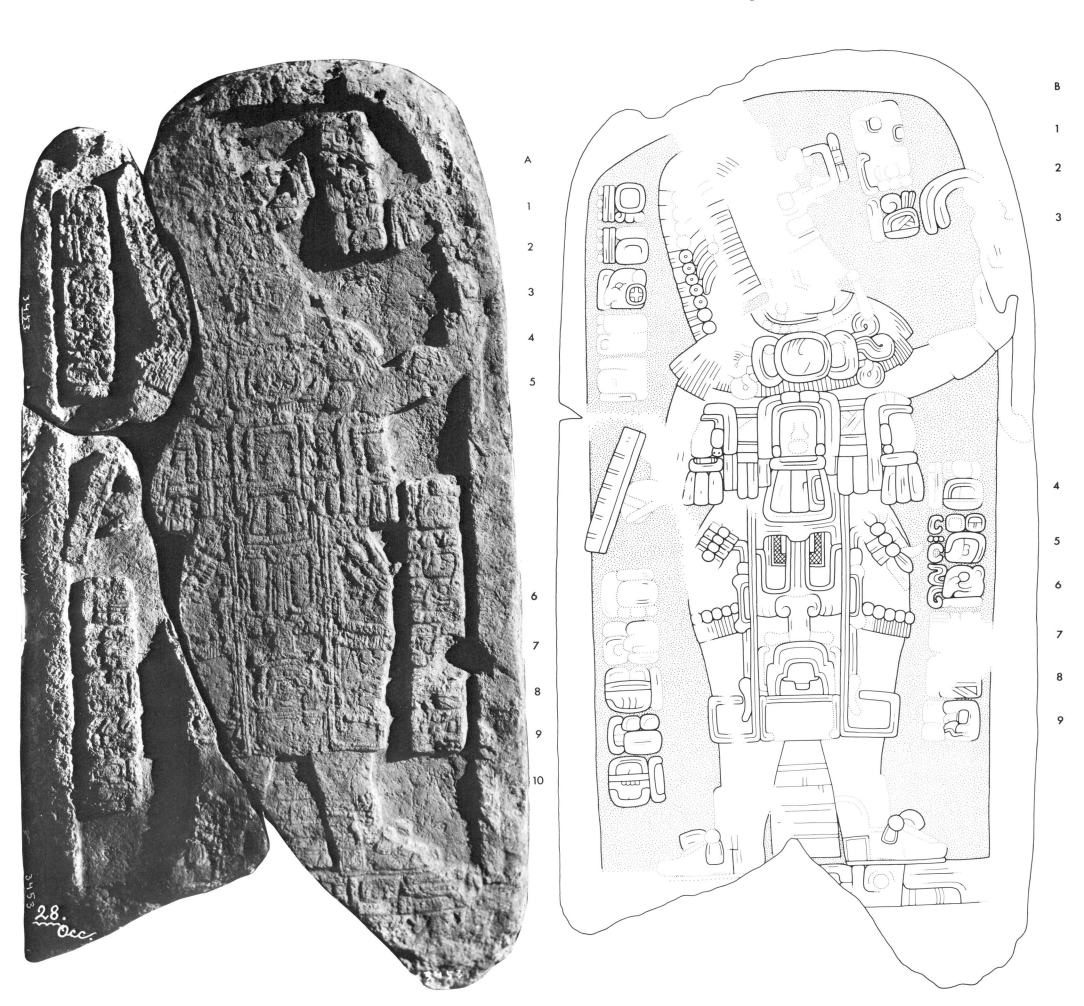

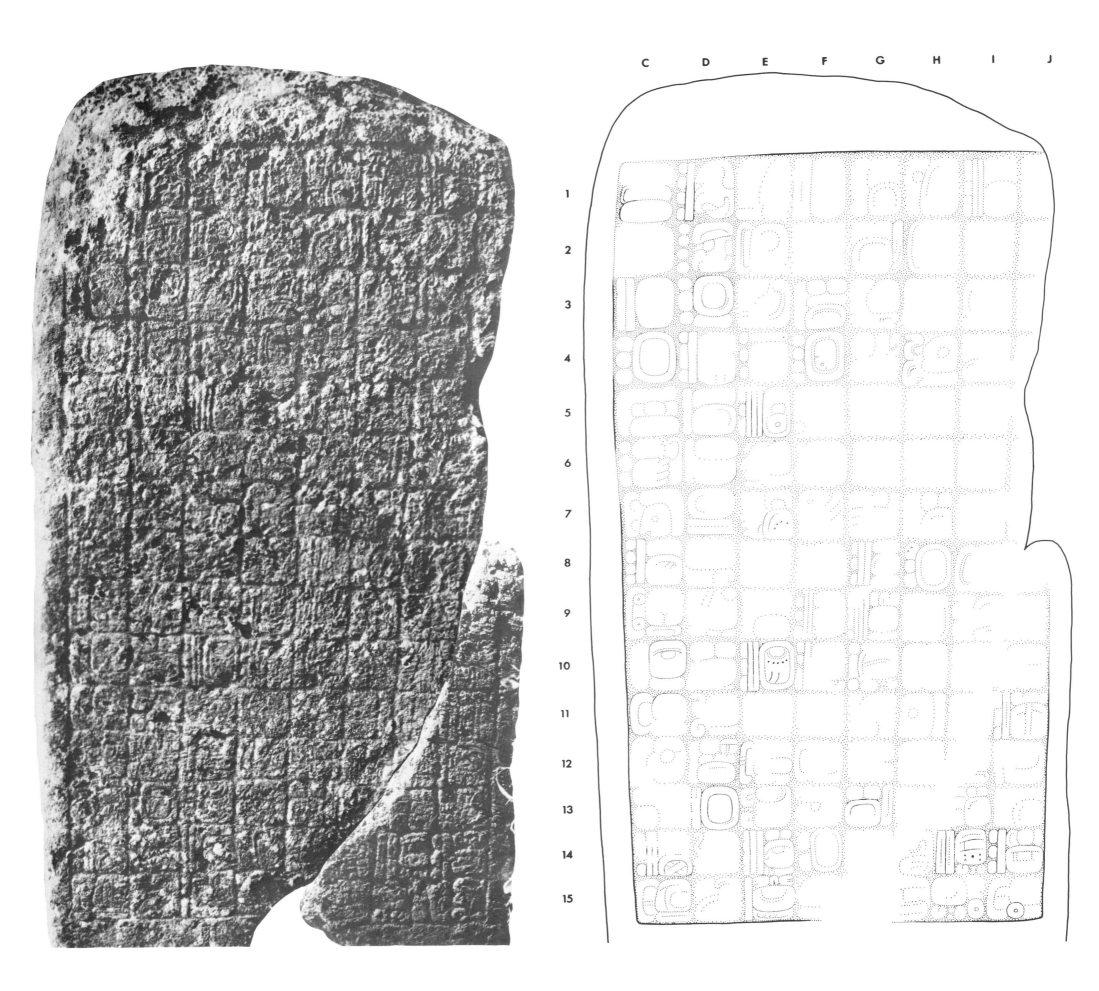

Back

Naranjo, Stela 29

LOCATION   Second from the north end of the front row of stelae that were set on the terrace at the foot of Structure C-9. Found by Maler lying on its right-hand edge, partly buried in debris. Removed to Melchor de Mencos in 1972.

CONDITION   Unbroken. The left-hand side of the front surface and the corresponding area of the back have deteriorated as the result of exposure to the weather.

MATERIAL   Limestone.

SHAPE   Nearly parallel sides, tapering slightly below the middle; rounded top.

DIMENSIONS
HLC	2.44 m
PB	0.76 m
MW	1.03 m
WBC	0.92 m
MTh	0.35 m
Rel	2.0 cm

CARVED AREAS   Front and back.

PHOTOGRAPHS   Reproduced from Maler's original negatives of 1905.

DRAWINGS   Graham, based on field drawings corrected by artificial light.

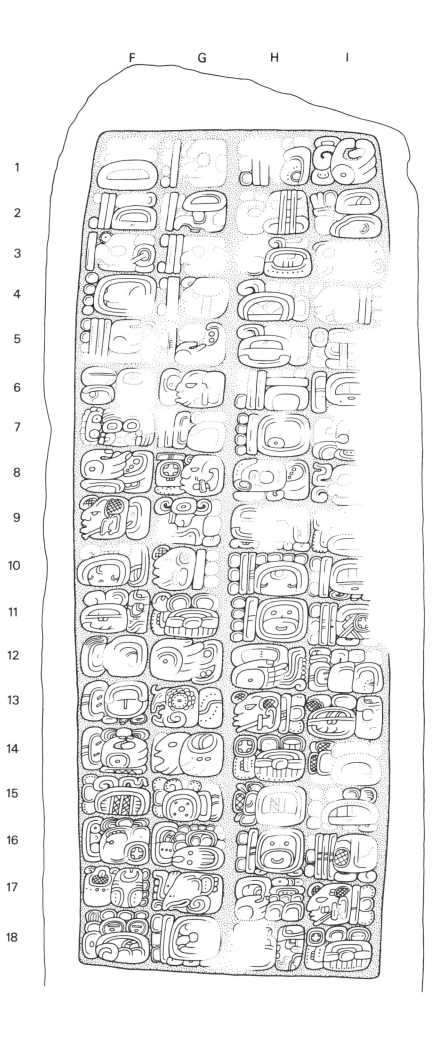

Back

Naranjo, Stela 30

LOCATION Second from the right-hand (southern) end in the front row of four stelae on the terrace at the foot of Structure C-9. In about 1966 looters broke up the stela, and two years later the fragments constituting the front surface came to light in the U.S. Customs at Houston, Texas, in a crate marked "Machinery." Through court action the government of Guatemala regained possession of these fragments.

CONDITION The stela had fallen forward and lay unbroken when discovered by Maler. The front was in practically perfect condition, the back considerably eroded. Since being smashed up by looters, the front is crisscrossed with breaks but has retained most of its fine detail. The back lies in a thousand chips at the site.

MATERIAL Fine-grained limestone.

SHAPE Parallel sides with nearly flat top.

DIMENSIONS
HLC	2.33 m
PB	0.87 m
MW	1.17 m
WBC	1.13 m
MTh	0.38 m
Rel	2.9 cm

CARVED AREAS Front and back.

PHOTOGRAPHS Reproduced from Maler's original negatives of 1905.

DRAWINGS Graham. Drawing of the front based on Maler's photograph and examination of the reassembled fragments; that of the back based on Maler's and Morley's photographs.

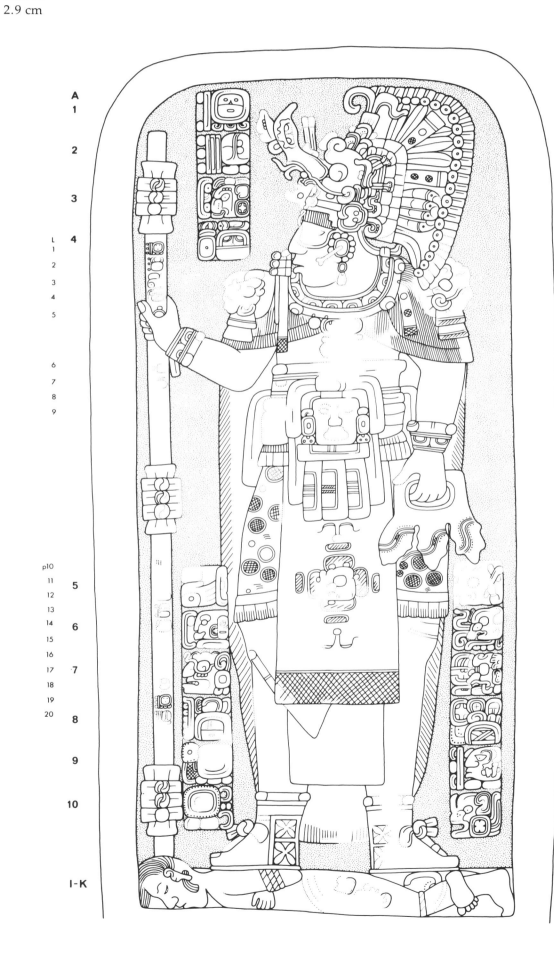

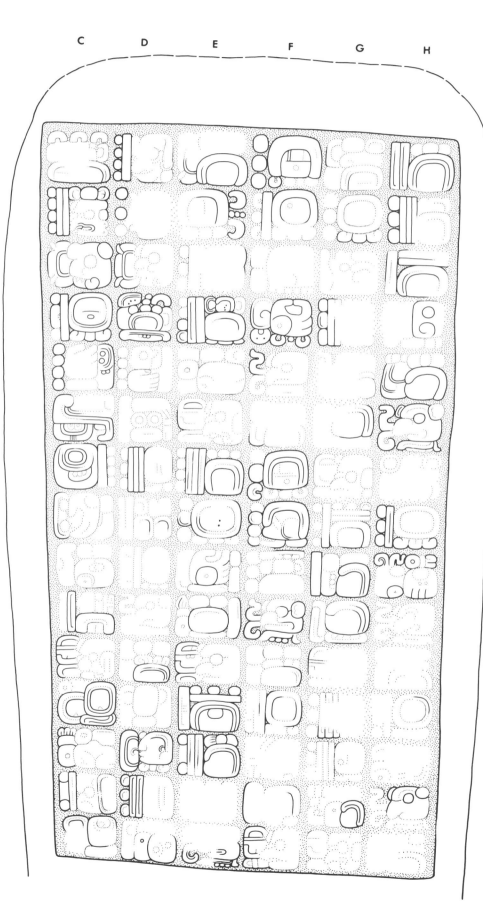

Back

Details

Naranjo, Stela 31

LOCATION   Southernmost stela in the front row of four set on the terrace built out from the foot of Structure C-9 on its west side. Removed to Flores in 1972.

CONDITION   Lying broken in three pieces when found by Maler, the front moderately eroded, the back more seriously so.

MATERIAL   Limestone.

SHAPE   The sides, nearly parallel in the upper half, taper somewhat toward the bottom. The top is flat.

DIMENSIONS
HLC	2.43 m (2.12 m measured on the back	
PB	0.35 m plus	
MW	1.19 m	
WBC	1.02 m	
MTh	0.31 m	
Rel	2.6 cm	

CARVED AREAS   Front and back.

PHOTOGRAPHS   Front: reproduced from Maler's original negative of 1905. Back: Morley, 1921.

DRAWINGS   Graham, based on field drawings corrected by artificial light.

REMARKS   8 cm below the foot of the sculptured panel there is a noticeable horizontal ledge. This may correspond with the floor level in the original setting.

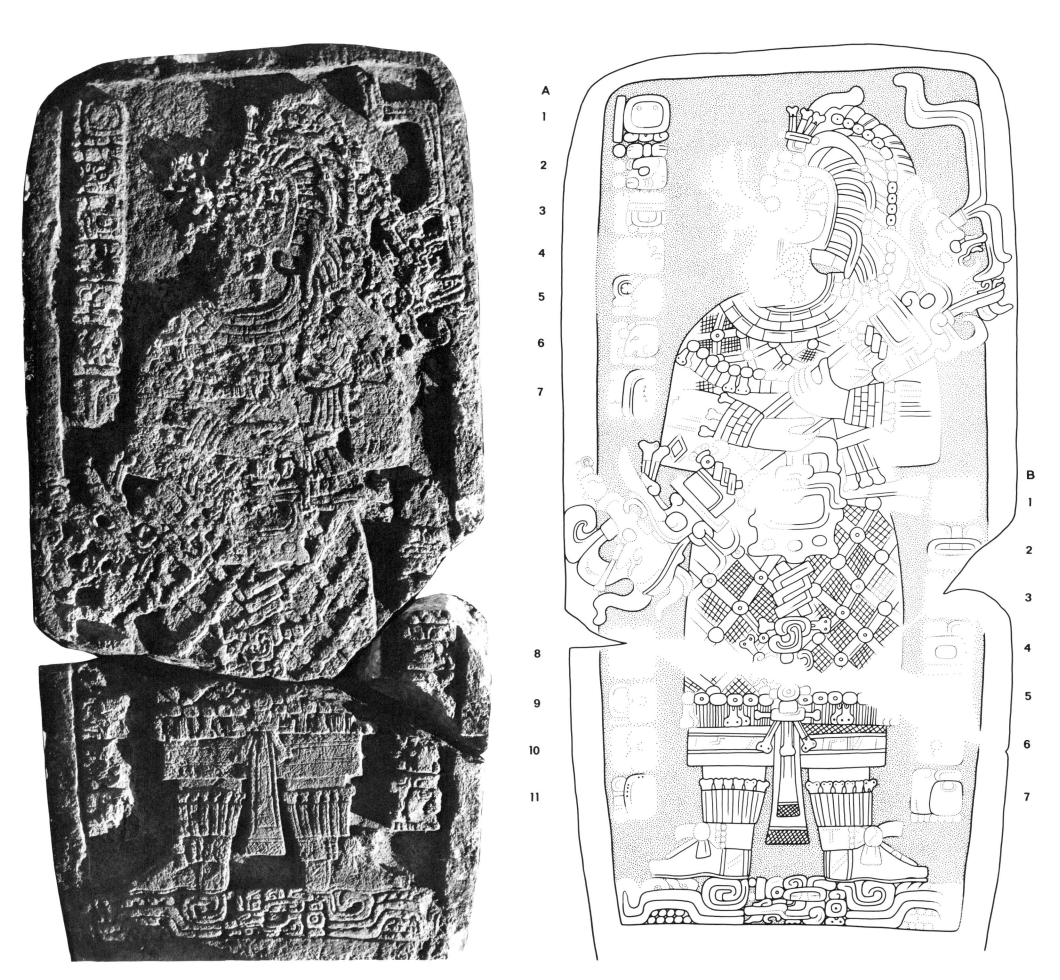

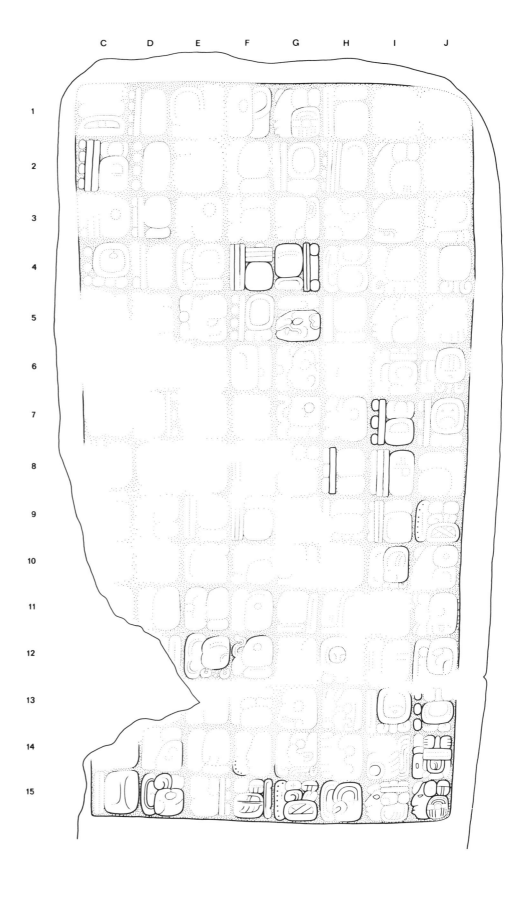

Back

Naranjo, Stela 32

LOCATION   Found by Maler lying face down on the plaza floor, at the foot of the terrace of Structure C-9, from which he considered that it must have fallen. It is perhaps more likely that it had been set up in the plaza, close to the place where Maler found it. Removed to Melchor de Mencos in 1972.

CONDITION   The top right-hand corner had been broken off when Maler discovered the stela. Although much of the sculptured surface was extremely well preserved, about one-quarter of it had flaked away. Looters in the mid-1960s thoroughly cracked the stela, possibly by means of fire and water, with the evident intention of removing it in pieces. This they never did.

MATERIAL   Fine-grained limestone.

SHAPE   Almost parallel-sided, with an irregular, flattish top.

DIMENSIONS
HLC	1.86 m
PB	0.83 m
MW	1.23 m
WBC	1.09 m
MTh	0.35 m
Rel	1.5 cm

CARVED AREAS   Front only.

PHOTOGRAPH   Reproduced from Maler's original negative of 1905.

DRAWING   Graham, based on a field drawing corrected by artificial light, making use also of photographs taken by Morley.

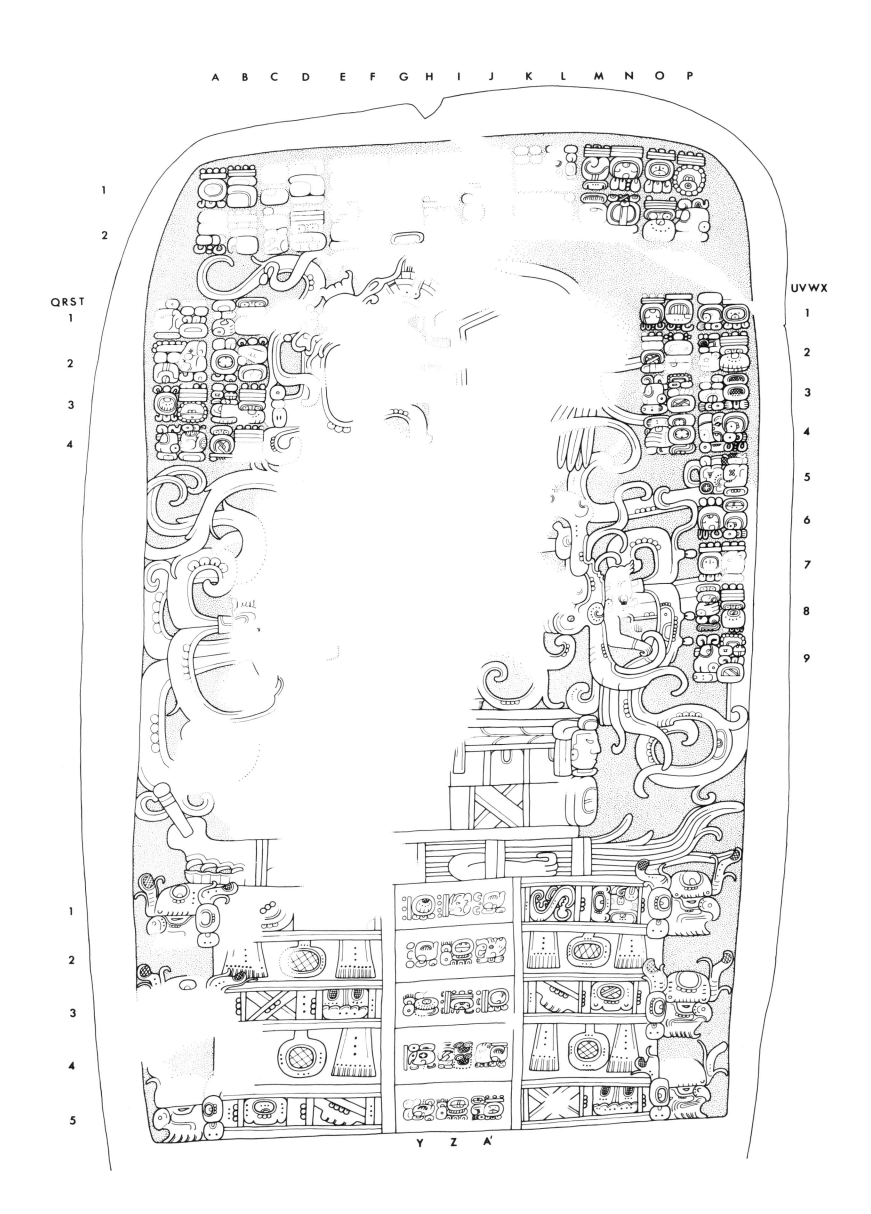

Naranjo, Stela 33

LOCATION   Northernmost of a group of three stelae in front, i.e., to the east, of Structure B-20. Removed to Melchor de Mencos in 1971.

CONDITION   Unbroken, with its sculptured surface moderately well-preserved.

MATERIAL   Gray, partially metamorphosed limestone, coarse-textured, and weathered brown on the surface.

SHAPE   Narrow shaft with a rounded peak, of oval cross section.

DIMENSIONS
HLC	1.83 m
PB	0.50 m
MW	0.45 m
WBC	0.45 m
MTh	0.30 m
Rel	1.2 cm

CARVED AREAS   Front only.

PHOTOGRAPHS   Graham, 1970.

DRAWING   Graham, based on a field drawing corrected by artificial light.

Details

Naranjo, Stela 34

LOCATION   In the center of a row of three on the west side of Structure B-20.

CONDITION   Unbroken but very much eroded, especially along certain bedding planes that intersect the surface.

MATERIAL   Coarse limestone of brownish color, with abundant inclusions of quartzite.

SHAPE   Narrow shaft with parallel sides; the top perhaps squared off originally.

DIMENSIONS
HLC	2.90 m
PB	0.91 m
MW	0.66 m
WBC	0.56 m
MTh	0.32 m
Rel	1.0 cm

CARVED AREAS   Front only.

PHOTOGRAPHS   Entire stela: Morley, 1921; detail: Graham, 1972.

Detail

Naranjo, Stela 35

LOCATION   Found by one of Morley's workers on the east side of Structure C-4, lying face up. Removed to Flores in 1971.

CONDITION   As found, the stela lay in five pieces, the smallest of which could not be found in 1971; this carried portions of glyphs C8, 9, 10. A fragment affecting glyphs E1, F1, also broke off the stela before discovery and has not come to light. The front is quite badly eroded, the back moderately so.

MATERIAL   Hard white limestone.

SHAPE   Sides nearly parallel; top unsymmetrical, with a shoulder caused by an ir- regularity of the shaft as quarried. The cross section is lenticular.

DIMENSIONS   HLC   1.40 m
             PB   0.48 (front)
                    0.61 m (back)
             MW   0.53 m
             WBC   0.48 m
             MTh   0.29 m
             Rel   1.2 cm

CARVED AREAS   Front and back.

PHOTOGRAPHS   Graham, 1973; Morley's 1921 photographs have been used for the small fragment that has disappeared since his day. The apparent discontinuity in the outline of the back is due to the lower portion having been photographed from an off-center camera position.

DRAWINGS   Graham. The drawings were based on tracings from photographs of flat casts made from latex molds. In this way distortion could be avoided: direct photographs of the stela suffer from unavoidable foreshortening toward the sides, due to the curvature of the sculptured surfaces. Details in the renderings were based on field drawings corrected by artificial light, and on Morley's photographs.

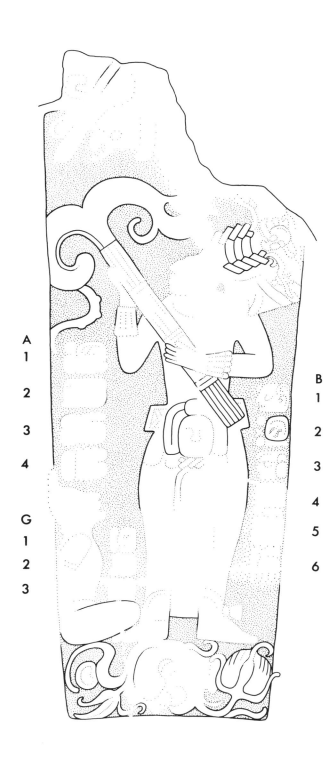

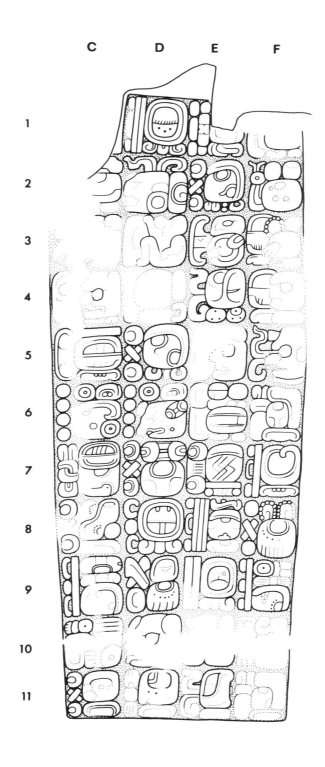

Back

Naranjo, Stela 36

LOCATION   Set up on the west side of the small structure B-1, which appears to have been associated with the ceremonial causeway leading north to Group D.

CONDITION   Intact and erect until February 1971. Then it was cracked into pieces by fire and the carved portion removed by some ignorant would-be merchant of pre-Columbian sculpture.

MATERIAL   A hard limestone.

SHAPE   Somewhat asymmetrically tapered, with a rounded top. Morley's photographs, the only ones known, were not taken from directly in front of the stela and so distort the shape.

DIMENSIONS   Ht   1.22m
             MW   0.76 m
             MTh   0.30 m
             Rel   unknown

CARVED AREAS   Front only.

PHOTOGRAPH   Morley, 1922.

DRAWING   von Euw, based on Morley's photograph, partially rectified in order to reduce distortion.

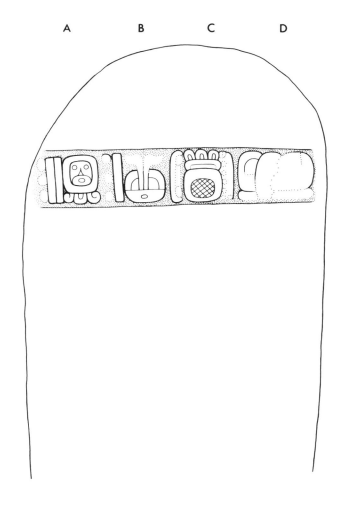

Naranjo, Stela 37

LOCATION   Isolated, near the edge of the plaza defined by Structures A-19, A-15, and the West Acropolis. In 1972 the fragments were removed to Flores.

CONDITION   Broken into several pieces of which six are known. The sculptured surface is quite badly eroded.

MATERIAL   Coarse-grained limestone.

SHAPE   Approximately parallel sides, narrowing slightly towards the top, which is nearly flat.

DIMENSIONS   HLC   2.88 m approx.
PB   unknown
MW   0.95 m
WBC   0.94 m approx.
MTh   0.50 m
Rel   2.2 cm

CARVED AREAS   Front only.

PHOTOGRAPH   Graham, 1971.

DRAWING   Graham, based on field drawing corrected by artificial light.

REMARKS   Stela 37 came to light in 1959 when it was struck by the blade of a bulldozer that was opening a road for lumbering. It was seen lying by the roadside, with scars still fresh, by Graham when he passed by soon after.

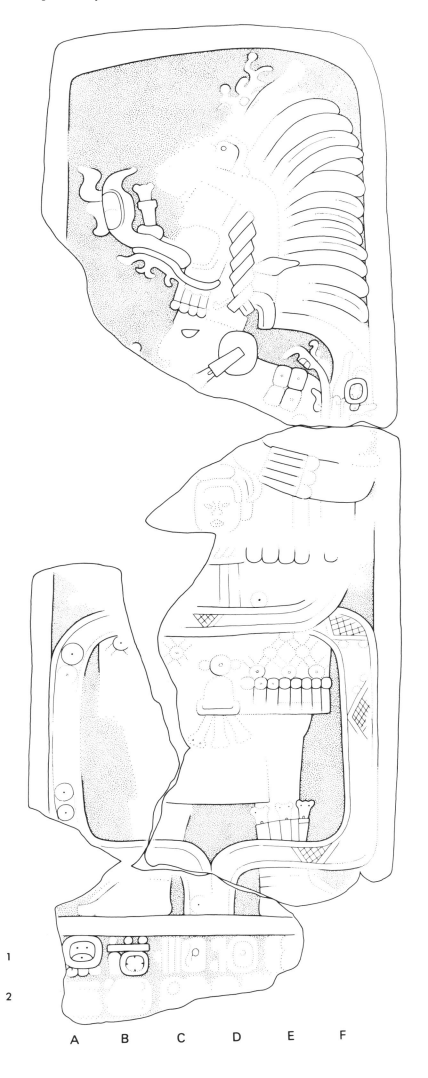

1

2

A   B   C   D   E   F

Naranjo, Stela 38

LOCATION Close against the south side of Structure D-1, 1.4 m to the west of Stela 39. When found, the butt was in situ, with the main portion of the stela resting on it and leaning forward against a tree. Rafael Morales H. excavated the butt and removed the stela to Flores in 1971.

CONDITION Broken into two pieces, with a clean break near the bottom of the sculptured panel. The degree of erosion is very slight, the face of the personage portrayed having been obliterated in antiquity.

MATERIAL A hard, fine-grained limestone.

SHAPE Somewhat barrel-shaped, with a rounded, flattish top.

DIMENSIONS

HLC	1.58	m
PB	0.58	m
MW	0.89	m
WBC	0.79	m
MTh	0.43	m
Rel	0.9	cm

CARVED AREAS Front surface only; carved in relief, with the inscriptions incised on raised panels.

PHOTOGRAPHS Graham, 1971.

DRAWING Graham, based on a field drawing corrected by artificial light.

Naranjo, Stela 39

LOCATION   Easternmost of two stelae at the foot of the stairway leading up the south side of Structure D-1. Discovered in 1971, the stela was stolen within the following year before it had been properly recorded.

CONDITION   Only the badly weathered lower portion was found, still set in the ground.

MATERIAL   Limestone.

SHAPE   Unknown.

DIMENSIONS   No measurements were taken; the shaft was narrow.

CARVED AREAS   The front alone seemed to have been carved.

PHOTOGRAPH   Graham, 1971.

Naranjo, Stela 40

LOCATION South side of Structure D-1, where it appears to have been set directly in front of Stela 39. Discovered in 1971 and removed in that year to the Museo Nacional de Antropología y Etnología, Guatemala City.

CONDITION Only the lower portion of the stela was found. It lay almost buried, face down, and so escaped erosion.

MATERIAL Limestone of reddish brown cast.

SHAPE Unknown.

DIMENSIONS

HLC	0.74 m plus
PB	0.40 m
MW	0.69 m
WBC	0.63 m
MTh	0.21 m
Rel	1.0 cm

CARVED AREAS Front only.

PHOTOGRAPH Graham, 1971.

DRAWING Graham, based on a field drawing corrected by artificial light.

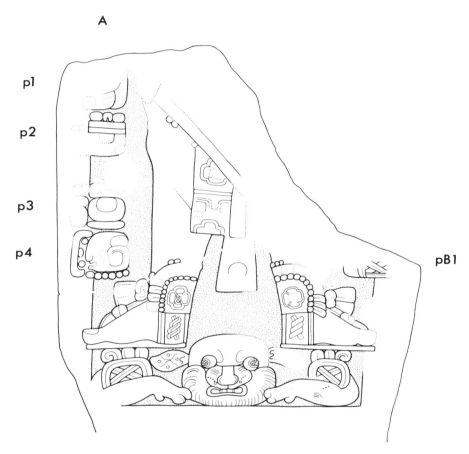

Naranjo, Altar 1

LOCATION This altar came to light in 1977 in the collection of Sr. Jorge Castillo, of Guatemala City. As a piece without secure provenience, it would ordinarily have been given a "Collections" designation; however, it can be recognized, on the basis of parallel passages in the two inscriptions, as almost certainly the altar of Stela 38 from Naranjo. Presumably it was removed from its setting not long before April 1971, the date of the first visit to Group D by Sr. Rafael Morales H. and the author, for on that occasion signs of recent activity by looters were in evidence.

CONDITION Broken into four pieces, plus a small fragment now lost. Apart from some losses by flaking, the surface condition is good. Red paint can be seen in some of the drilled holes.

MATERIAL Yellowish limestone of fine grain, flawed by weak cleavage planes.

SHAPE Oval, with smoothly dressed face and (to a lesser extent) edges.

DIMENSIONS
Max. diameter	0.82	m
Min. diameter	0.61	m
MTh	0.14	m
Rel	0.2	cm

CARVED AREAS Upper surface only; text incised, with central cartouche outlined in slightly greater relief.

PHOTOGRAPH Graham, 1977.

DRAWING Graham, based on a drawing corrected by artificial light.

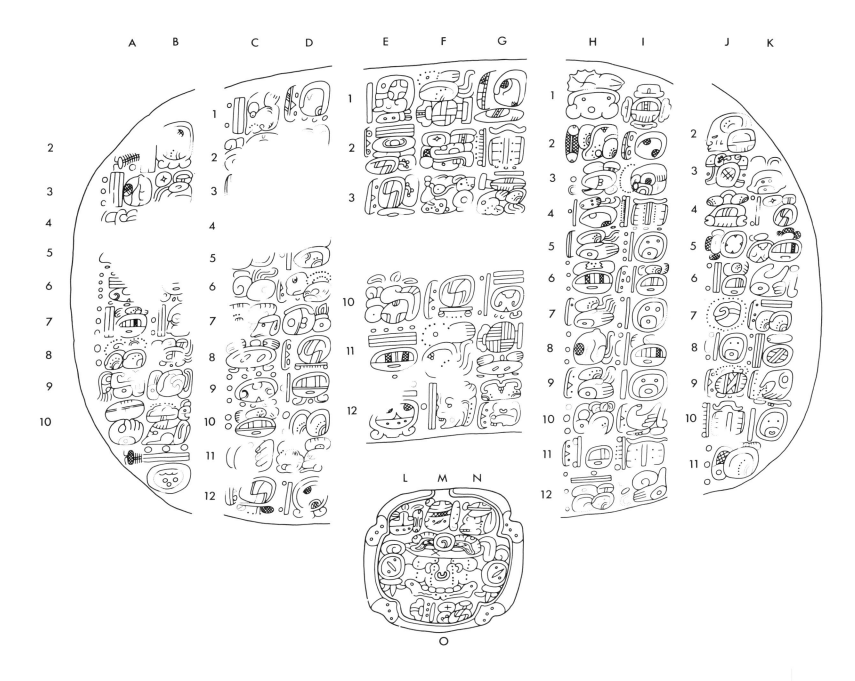

Naranjo, Lintel 1

LOCATION   Found by Maler reused in the second step of the Hieroglyphic Stairway, between Inscription 7 and Inscription 8 in Morley's terminology, or Step VII and Step VIII in the informal usage of this work. Removed by Herbert J. Spinden to the American Museum of Natural History in 1914.

CONDITION   Found by Maler buried in debris and rather well preserved, although trimmed down from its original size. Already cracked, Spinden broke the lintel to carry it away; this action resulted in no significant loss of detail. Textual evidence shows that a whole column of glyphs was anciently trimmed off the left side, and half a column on the right. Maler was probably mistaken in supposing the upper border also to have been trimmed before reuse in the stairway.

MATERIAL   Limestone.

SHAPE   Essentially rectangular, with a narrow, well-finished border above and one that is wider and more roughly dressed below.

DIMENSIONS
Ht	0.47 m
MW	0.70 m
HSc	0.37 m
MTh	unknown
Rel	unknown

CARVED AREAS   Front only (or underside, if truly a lintel).

PHOTOGRAPH   Reproduced from Maler's original negative of 1905.

DRAWING   Graham, based on Maler's photograph and on a drawing made of the original lintel on display, mounted in a showcase from which it was evidently not convenient to remove it.

REMARKS   This piece might better have been called Panel 1. The fact that inscriptions on lintels generally run down rather than across and the inequality of the borders suggest a panel, one perhaps that had its lower edge set in a floor. A further point is that carved stone lintels are otherwise unknown in the eastern Maya lowlands.

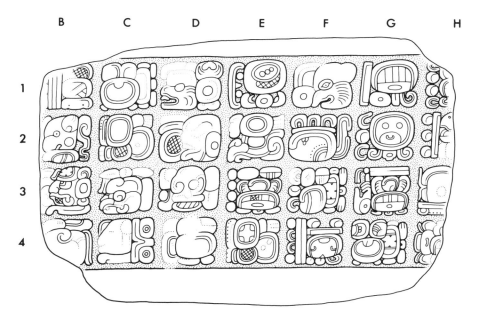

Naranjo, Hieroglyphic Stairway

A NOTE ON NOMENCLATURE   Maler's numbering of the individual blocks, or Inscriptions in Morley's terminology, is retained but given in Roman numerals. Formally a block will be referred to as HS. 1, IV, for example, or less formally as Step IV where there is no danger of confusion with the fourth step of the stairway.

LOCATION   The carved blocks were incorporated into the lower part of the stairway leading up the west side of Structure B-18. Alterations to the stairway and dismemberment of it evidently began long ago, probably in Postclassic times, as Maler realized when he found a reused panel inserted in place of a broken step. Another striking piece of evidence is the step, undoubtedly once part of the stairway and here designated Step XIII, that was found at Ucanal, 35 kilometers away as the guacamayo flies.

As mentioned above in the general description of the site, the stairway was picked clean of its sculpture within fifteen years of discovery, except for the three monsters' heads, and they disappeared in the 1960s. The location of the steps in 1977 is as follows: Steps I and IV to XI in the British Museum; Step XII in the Museum of the American Indian, Heye Foundation, New York City; Step XIII in storage at Tikal National Park; Steps II and III lost, the lat-

ter possibly in transit to El Cayo in 1920 (Morley 1937-38, vol. 2, p. 58).

CONDITION   The general condition of the steps at the time of their discovery was good because they were of hard stone, and most of them had fallen on their faces or else had been buried in debris. Step XIII retains most of its design in spite of having lain face up for a few centuries, at least. The only noteworthy breakage, apart from Step VIII, the left-hand half of which is missing, is the loss of about one-tenth of the cartouche of Step XI. As the result of being broken up for removal, the steps now in the British Museum show some small losses. Step XII appears exactly as in Maler's photograph, and Step XIII was taken out of Ucanal entire.

MATERIAL   Hard, fine-grained limestone.

SHAPE   Rectangular blocks, with the front and upper surfaces smoothly dressed. The upper edge is well rounded in some cases, most notably Steps IV, VII, and XIII, and least so in Steps V and VI.

DIMENSIONS   The most consistent dimensions are those of the cartouches: these all fall within one centimeter of 0.35 by 0.38 m for the smaller steps, neglecting the surrounding line. The width of the stone

blocks is more variable and in some cases cannot now be established because of breakage. The two larger blocks, Steps V and VI, have cartouches measuring 0.75 by 0.60 m and 0.78 by 0.62 m respectively.

CARVED AREAS   Front surfaces (risers) only.

PHOTOGRAPHS   Steps I to XII: reproduced from Maler's original negatives of 1905; Step XIII: Graham, 1972.

DRAWINGS   Graham, based on the above photographs and drawings from the originals (excepting Steps II and III). The outlines of some of the blocks have been left incomplete because they fell outside the frame of Maler's photograph and have since been altered by breakage.

The diagram showing the arrangement of the steps and the monsters' heads is taken from Morley 1937-38, vol. 2, fig. 26. Individual blocks are numbered in Arabic numerals on the diagram, rather than in the Roman numerals employed in this work.

NOTE   Further information on Step XIII will be found in the section of this work treating of Ucanal and its monuments.

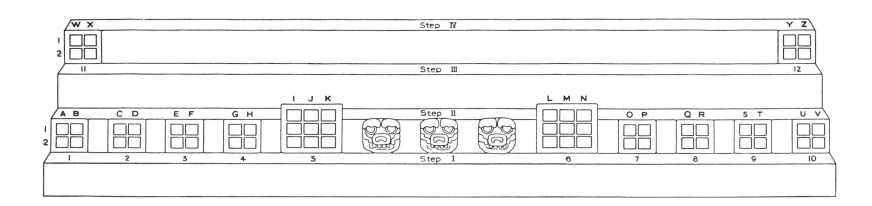

Step I

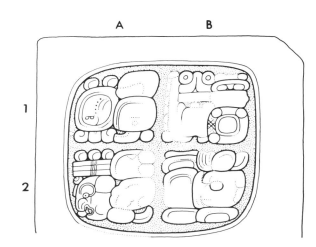

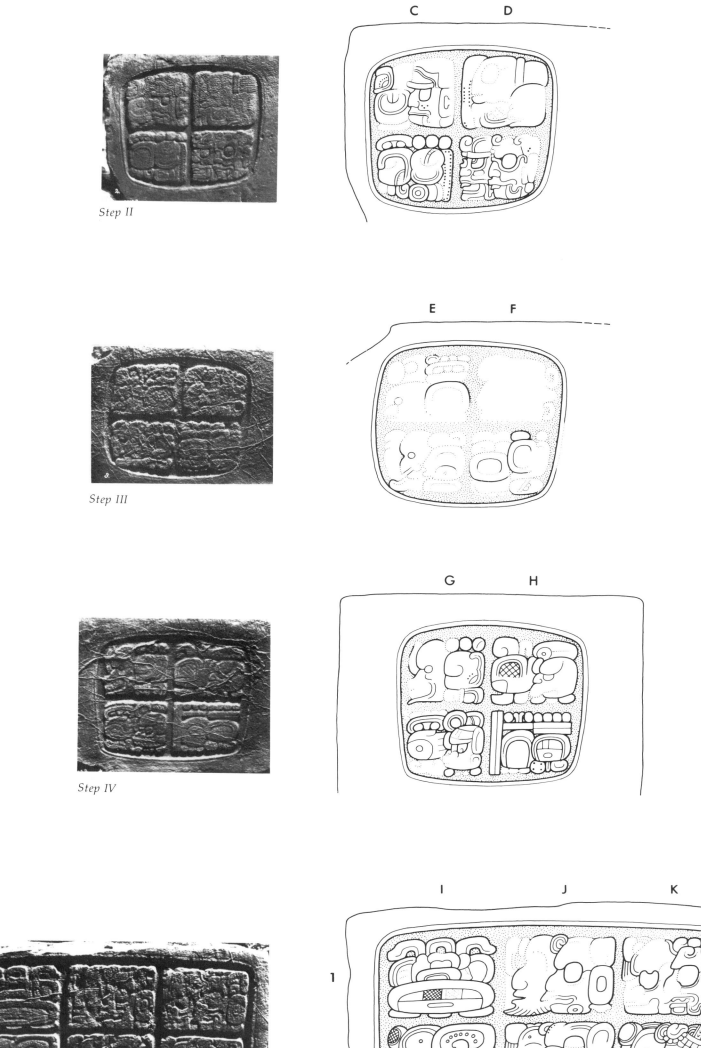

Step II

Step III

Step IV

Step V

L M N

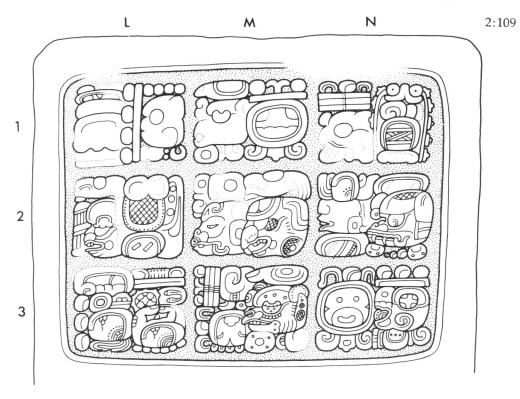

1

2

3

Step VI

O P

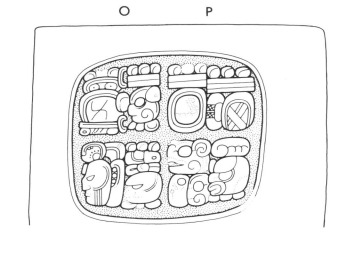

Step VII

R

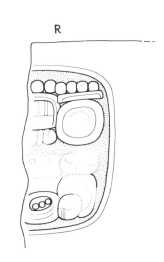

Step VIII

S T

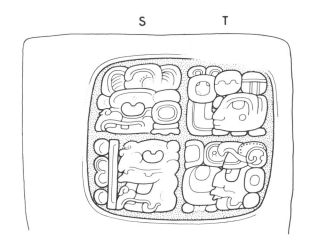

Step IX

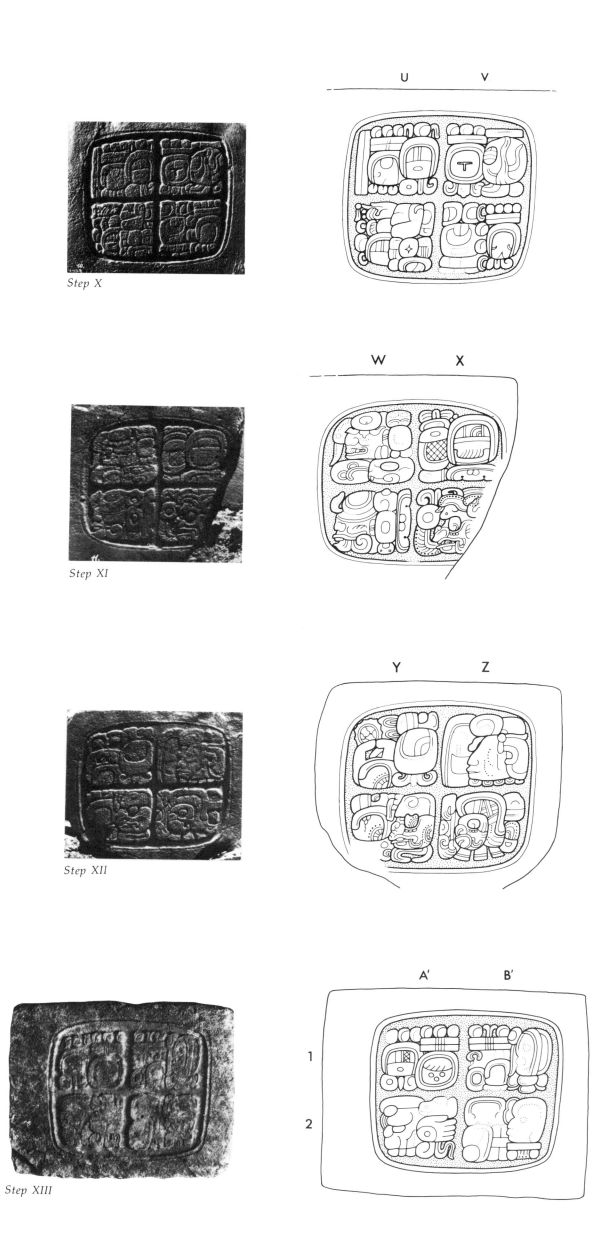

Step X

Step XI

Step XII

Step XIII

Addenda for Naranjo

Suggestions have been received that a listing of dates for the monuments included in this work would be useful. In response to these requests, we intend to offer such information on an occasional basis.

The following list of Naranjo dates is taken from an unpublished study of texts at this site by Peter Mathews, who has kindly consented to its publication here. In each case the date given is the latest recorded, except in those instances where such a date clearly postdates the piece, as does the mention of 10.0.0.0 7 Ahau 18 Zip on Altar 1, at K6-K7.

St. 1	(F5-E6)	9.13.10. 0. 0	7 Ahau	3 Cumku
St. 2	(B1-B9)	9.14. 1. 3.19	3 Cauac	2 Pop
St. 3	(E4-E5)	9.14. 1. 3.19	3 Cauac	2 Pop
St. 4		unknown		
St. 5	(A1-A2)	9.13. 7. 3. 8	9 Lamat	1 Zotz
St. 6	(A1-A2)	9.18.17. 5.18	9 Etznab	11 Muan
St. 7	(A4)	9.19. 0. 3. 0	4 Ahau	18 Zac
St. 8	(C1-C9)	9.18.10. 0. 0	10 Ahau	8 Zac
St. 9		unknown		
St. 10	(A10)	9.19. 0. 3. 0	4 Ahau	18 Zac
St. 11	(A1-A2)	*9.18.13. 3.13	6 Ben	6 Kankin
St. 12	(F12-G12)	9.18.10. 0. 0	10 Ahau	8 Zac
St. 13	(E1-F9)	9.17.10. 0. 0	12 Ahau	8 Pax
St. 14	(A1-A4)	9.18. 0. 0. 0	11 Ahau	18 Mac
St. 15		unknown		
St. 16		unknown		
St. 17		unknown		
St. 18	(I5-J6)	9.14.15. 0. 0	11 Ahau	18 Zac
St. 19	(A1-B2)	9.17.10. 0. 0	12 Ahau	8 Pax
St. 20	(A1-A2)	9.14. 2.12.16	7 Cib	14 Chen
St. 21	(E9-E10)	9.13.15. 0. 0	13 Ahau	18 Pax
St. 22	(G19-H20)	9.13.10. 0. 0	7 Ahau	3 Cumku
St. 23	(G17-H18)	9.14. 0. 0. 0	6 Ahau	13 Muan
St. 24	(E14-D16)	9.13.10. 0. 0	7 Ahau	3 Cumku
St. 25	(C9-D10)	9. 9. 2. 0. 4	12 Kan	17 Zip
St. 26		unknown		
St. 27		9. 9.10. 0. 0	(approximately)	
St. 28	(J12-J13)	9.14.10. 0. 0	5 Ahau	3 Mac
St. 29	(H11-I12)	9.13. 3. 0. 0	9 Ahau	13 Pop
St. 30	(H12-G14)	9.14. 3. 0. 0	7 Ahau	18 Kankin
St. 31	(I13-J14)	9.14.10. 0. 0	5 Ahau	3 Mac
St. 32	(A '5b)	9.19.10. 0. 0	8 Ahau	8 Xul
St. 33	(A1-B1)	9.17.10. 0. 0	12 Ahau	8 Pax
St. 34		unknown		
St. 35	(E9-F9)	9.18.10. 0. 0	10 Ahau	8 Zac
St. 36	(A1-B1)	9.17.10. 0. 0	12 Ahau	8 Pax
St. 37		unknown		
St. 38	(B2-B7)	9. 8. 0. 0. 0	5 Ahau	3 Chen
St. 39		unknown		
St. 40		unknown		
Alt. 1	(K10-J11)	*9. 8. 0. 0. 0	5 Ahau	3 Chen
Lnt. 1	(G2-H3)	9.10. 0. 0. 0	1 Ahau	8 Kayab
HS	(I1-K3)	9.10.10. 0. 0	13 Ahau	18 Kankin

*Dates not taken from Mathews

p.2:5, Area map (also p.3:5 and p.4:8). Lest any readers of early volumes of the *Corpus* betake themselves to the Bay of Bengal in search of Maya ruins reported to exist in that part of the world, attention is drawn to an error in the longitudes marked on those area maps: "W" should be substituted for "E."

p.2:9, Register of Inscriptions. Between "Stelae 1 to 40" and "Lintel 1," insert "Altar 1."

p.2:29, Naranjo, Stela 9. A number of fitting fragments of weathered sculpture, confiscated by Mexican authorities on some unknown occasion and stored at present by INAH in the Templo San Juan de Dios, Merida, prove to be part of Stela 9. The upper panel is missing, so too is the upper rear portion of the principal figure's headdress, the head and torso of the subsidiary standing figure, and the head of the captive.

No worthwhile details not apparent in our published drawing could be distinguished, except that the glyph panel close to the ruler's left leg resolves itself more clearly into three glyphs; not well enough, however, to merit publication of a new drawing. The maximum depth of relief on these fragments is 2.5 cm.

p.2:35, Naranjo, Stela 12. The front of this stela has come to light in Switzerland as the property of a Belgian collector. One of the pieces into which the front surface had been cut was evidently lost in transit. The loss, comprising the ruler's right foot and the captive from the waist up, has been restored on the basis of Maler's photograph.

p.2:39, Naranjo, Stela 14. A small fragment from this stela has also been found in the Templo San Juan de Dios, Merida, whither it was brought after confiscation by the police. The fragment shows part of the featherwork at the bottom of the apron and part of the masks on the back of both sandals.

p.2:60, Naranjo, Stela 23. Peter Mathews has drawn my attention to a mistake in the drawing of glyph F8. The Initial Series date calls for 16 Uo, rather than 11 Uo, and three bars are indeed visible in the photograph and were also recorded in my field drawing.

Chunhuitz

LOCATION AND ACCESS

This very small ceremonial center lies close to the foot of the escarpment that runs east and west halfway across Peten. Against it have gathered the waters of Lakes Peten Itza, Yaxha, and Sacnab and the swamp near the ruins of Naranjo. To the northeast of that swamp, a few kilometers along the base of the escarpment, there is a smaller reed-covered swamp into which projects a low neck or peninsula stemming from the escarpment. Here stand the ruins of Chunhuitz.

The most certain route to the site is that indicated on the map reproduced on this page, although a more direct one from Bambonal is sometimes open. In any case, it is preferable to camp at Manantial where there is an unfailing little spring, rather than rely on the muddy waterholes closer to the ruins for the sake of avoiding a forty-five-minute walk.

PRINCIPAL INVESTIGATIONS AT THE SITE

In 1910 A.M. Tozzer and R.E. Merwin stopped near Chunhuitz and made a note of an outlying mound group, but failed to see the main group with its stela. The first archaeologist to do so was Sylvanus B. Morley, who spent a day there in June 1914. At Morley's request A. Ledyard Smith spent two days in the early 1930s making a sketch plan of the site. The published version of this (Morley 1937-38, vol. 5, pl. 210b) forms the basis of the plan given here, modified in ways suggested more by eye than by measurement.

REGISTER OF INSCRIPTIONS AT CHUNHUITZ

Stela 1

REFERENCES CITED

MORLEY, SYLVANUS G.
1937-38   *The Inscriptions of Peten.* Carnegie Institution of Washington, Publication 437, 5 vols. Washington, D.C.

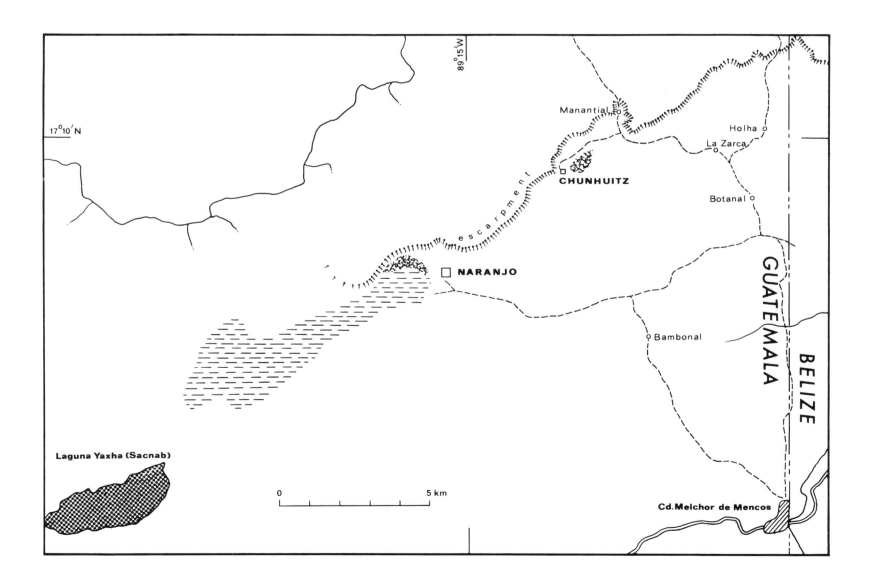

89°15′W

17°10′N

Manantial

Holha

La Zarca

CHUNHUITZ

Botanal

escarpment

NARANJO

Bambonal

GUATEMALA

BELIZE

Laguna Yaxha (Sacnab)

0   5 km

Cd. Melchor de Mencos

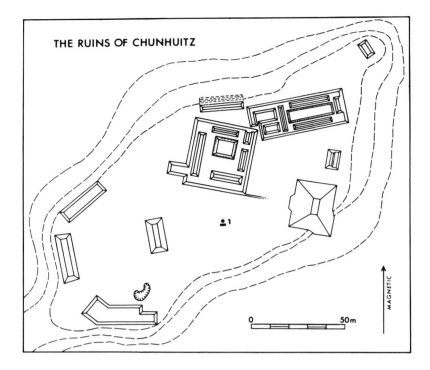

THE RUINS OF CHUNHUITZ

0   50 m

MAGNETIC

Chunhuitz, Stela 1

LOCATION Morley reported finding the stela standing near the middle of the irregular plaza area that is defined on three sides by mounds and on the fourth by the edge of the terraced ceremonial area. Since then the stela has fallen. Morley's mention of a circular altar "in front (north) of this stela" (Morley 1937-38, vol. 2, p. 228) is the only clue to its orientation.

CONDITION Broken into one large and three smaller pieces, as well as some fragments now lost. The design carved on the two sculptured faces is almost entirely weathered away.

MATERIAL A friable limestone breccia.

SHAPE Parallel sides, with the shape of the top unknown.

DIMENSIONS
HLC	2.12 m
PB	0.87 m
MW	0.84 m
WBC	0.77 m
MTh	0.30 m
Rel	2.0 cm

CARVED AREAS Front and back.

PHOTOGRAPHS Graham, 1971. The front aspect of the upper right-hand fragment was not photographed; the carving on it had in any case been completely eroded.

DRAWINGS Graham, based on field drawings corrected by artificial light.

REMARKS It appears that Morley did not see the pieces broken from the upper part of this stela.

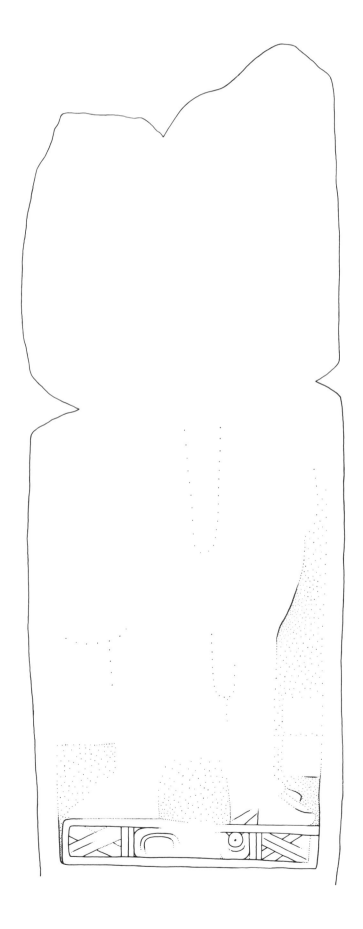

Back

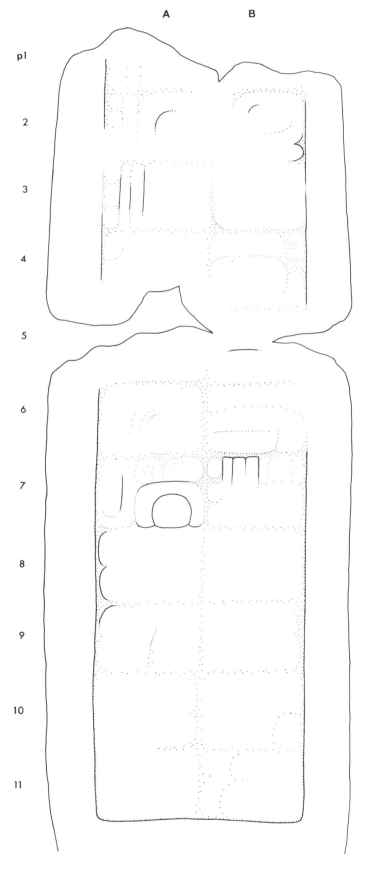

XUNANTUNICH

OTHER NAMES FOR THE SITE
Mount Maloney
Benque Viejo

Note: In Appendix A of volume 1 of this work, "Benque Viejo" is given as the preferred name for this site. But "Xunantunich," though less well established in the literature, has now been settled on by the Belize Department of Archaeology as the official name.

LOCATION AND ACCESS
Xunantunich is situated on the top of a steep hill overlooking the Río Mopan, or Western Branch, a tributary of the Belize River. It lies less than 2 km north of Benque Viejo town and at a like distance from the Maya town of Succotz. Access to the ruins is by vehicle ferry across the river at Succotz and thence by road into the plaza.

PRINCIPAL INVESTIGATIONS AT THE SITE
The earliest published account of these ruins is due to Thomas Gann (Gann 1893-95). In it, he describes seeing Stela 1 and its altar; and then, "behind the mounds, and hidden in the dense bush, we found another fragment with sculpture and hieroglyphics upon it, and near this two large oval stones each about 18 inches by 12 inches, and polished smooth, lying side by side." This fragment, which appears not to have been reported since, may have lain between Structure A-7 and Group B.

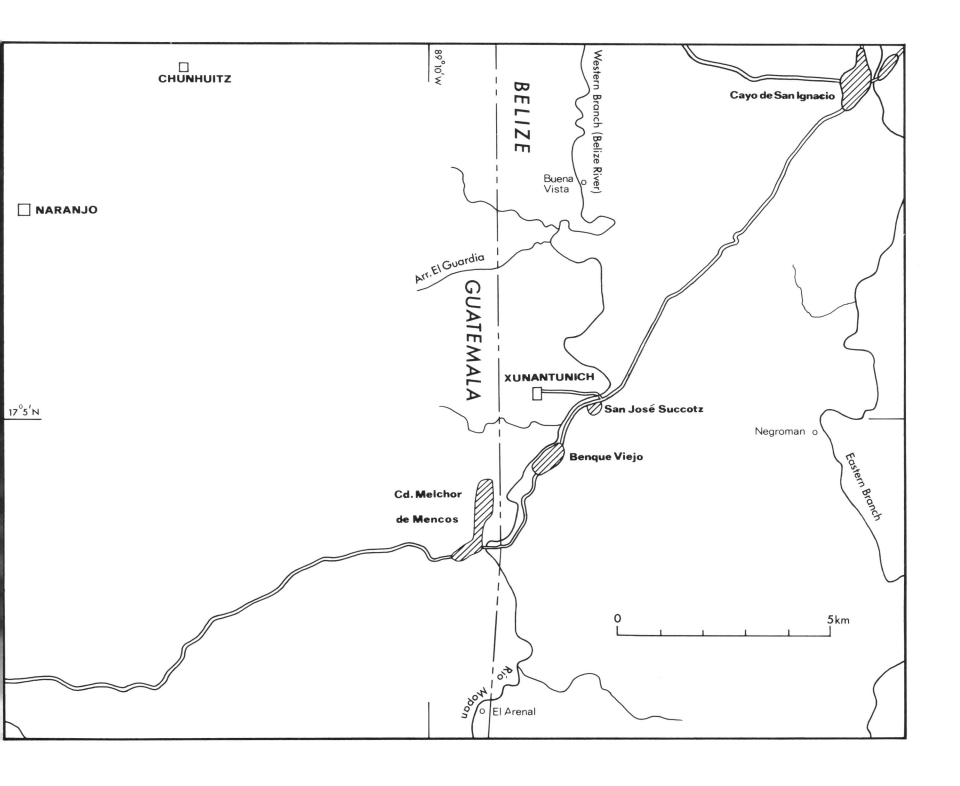

Teobert Maler visited the site briefly in 1905, and later published good photographs of Stela 1 and the altar, as well as a plan of Structure A-6 (Maler 1908, pp. 73-79).

Gann returned to the site in 1924. He sank pits into several mounds, including Structures A-3, A-7, and A-9 (Gann 1925) and dispatched Altar 1 to the British Museum, having, regrettably, first trimmed off the hieroglyphic inscription.

In 1938 J.E.S. Thompson spent three weeks at the site, excavating small structures in Group B (Thompson 1940).

A.H. Anderson, later to become Archaeological Commissioner for the colony, rediscovered in 1949 an area of stucco decoration on Structure A-6, which Gann had also noticed. This was cleared by Linton Satterthwaite the following year, and it proved to be the decorated upper zone of an earlier structure underlying the twelve-chambered "palace-type" building (Satterthwaite 1950).

Some excavations were evidently carried out in 1952 by Michael Stewart (Anderson 1952, p. 34), although no report on them seems to have been published. Seven years later, E.W. Mackie excavated Structures A-11 and A-15 (Mackie 1961).

In the late 1960s, Peter Schmidt, acting Archaeological Commissioner, was working at the site. He consolidated Structure A-6, arranged for the site to be mapped, and found the upper portion of a new carved stela, Stela 8, on the south side of Structure A-1, close to Stela 1. In 1973 his successor in the post, Joseph Palacio, cleared all of the debris from that side of the mound, revealing a row of monuments laid end to end. The lower portion of Stela 8 was among them and Stela 9.

NOTES ON THE RUINS

Morley's description of the site (Morley 1937-38, pp. 204-212) still has value when read in conjunction with the later reports cited above. Morley himself made two visits of only an hour's duration each in the years 1915 and 1920.

A NOTE ON THE PLAN OF THE RUINS

The published plan has been redrawn and adapted from two plans, one of contours and the other of structures, which were drawn by Walter J. Carbis of the Survey Department of Belize. These were based on his survey, made at the request of Peter Schmidt in 1969. Carbis gives the elevation of the top of Structure A-6 as 210 m.

Two small mounds within the plaza bounded by Structures A-10 to A-13 are not shown on our plan. These mounds, situated near the northwest and southeast corners of the plaza, are both marked "T" by Gann (1925, plate facing p. 60), while Morley calls them Structures XIV and XV, respectively (1937-38, pl. 191a).

REGISTER OF INSCRIPTIONS AT XUNANTUNICH

Stelae 1,8,9
Altar 1

REFERENCES CITED

ANDERSON, A. HAMILTON
   1952   "Archaeology in British Honduras Today," *Proceedings of the Thirtieth International Congress of Americanists, Held at Cambridge*, pp. 32-35. London.

GANN, THOMAS W.F.
   1893-95   "On Exploration of Two Mounds in British Honduras," *Proceedings*, Society of Antiquaries of London, n.s., vol. 15, pp. 430-434.
   1925   *Mystery Cities*. Duckworth, London.

MACKIE, EUAN W.
   1961   "New Light on the End of the Classic Maya Culture at Benque Viejo, British Honduras," *American Antiquity*, vol. 27, no. 2, pp. 216-224.

MALER, TEOBERT
1908 *Exploration in the Department of Peten, Guatemala, and Adjacent Region.* Memoirs of the Peabody Museum, Harvard University, vol. 4, no. 2. Cambridge, Massachusetts.

MORLEY, SYLVANUS G.
1937-38 *The Inscriptions of Peten.* Carnegie Institution of Washington, Publication 437, 5 vols. Washington, D.C.

SATTERTHWAITE, LINTON
1950 "Plastic Art of a Maya Palace," *Archaeology*, vol. 3, no. 4, pp. 215-222. Cambridge, Massachusetts.

THOMPSON, J. ERIC S.
1940 "Late Ceramic Horizons at Benque Viejo, British Honduras," Carnegie Institution of Washington, Publication 528. *Contributions to American Anthropology and History*, no. 35. Washington, D.C.

CORRIGENDA CONCERNING
XUNANTUNICH FOR VOLUME 1

p.1:23, After "Benque Viejo" delete "BVJ" and substitute "see Xunantunich." After "Xunantunich" delete "see Benque Viejo" and substitute "XUN."

p.1:24, Delete "BVJ Benque Viejo." Insert "XUN Xunantunich" between XUL and XUP.

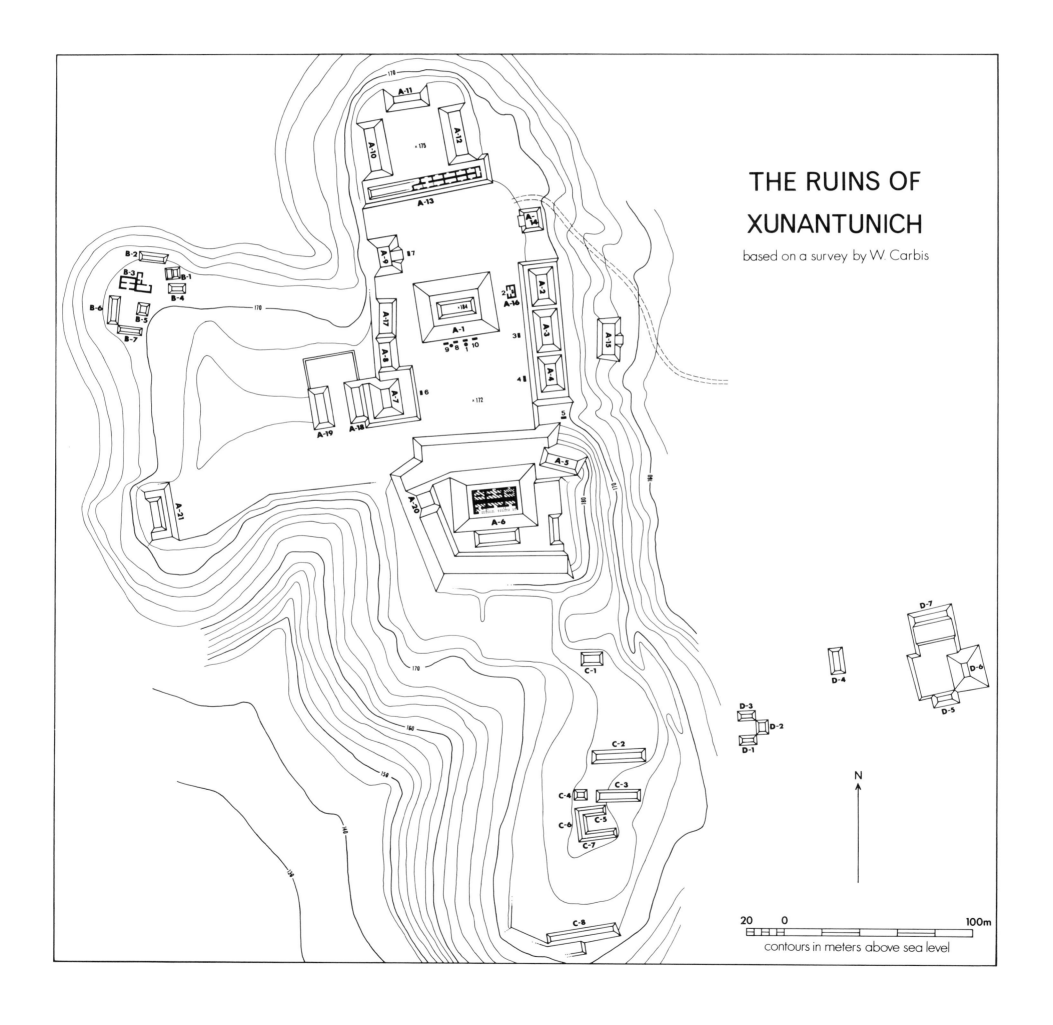

THE RUINS OF
XUNANTUNICH

based on a survey by W. Carbis

N

20   0   100m

contours in meters above sea level

Xunantunich, Stela 1

LOCATION   When found, the lower part of the stela was in situ on the south side of Structure A-6, not far from its center line; it was later excavated by Gann (Gann 1925, pp. 57, 66). The whole stela has recently been moved farther away from the mound and roofed over.

CONDITION   Broken into two large pieces and intermediate fragments. Most of the latter had disappeared prior to discovery, but three were recorded by Maler and Morley. The upper right-hand corner of the shaft has been broken since the time of Maler.

MATERIAL   Limestone.

SHAPE   Sides nearly parallel although somewhat bulging, and tapering markedly in the upper part; slanting top.

DIMENSIONS   HLC   3.30 m plus
PB   0.87 m
EPB   0.50 m
(Maler 1908, p. 79)
MW   1.26 m
WBC   1.18 m
MTh   0.40 m
Rel   8.0 cm

CARVED AREAS   Front only.

PHOTOGRAPH   Graham, 1976, with insertion of fragments from negatives by Maler and Morley.

DRAWING Graham, based on field drawing corrected by artificial light. The outline of the right-hand edges of glyphs B3 and B4 is taken from Thompson's field notes (Peabody Museum Archives, CIW 214, p. 57). Thompson sketched only the left-hand edge of some fragment, but it seems possible that this was the same fragment that Maler included in his photograph, placed in such a way as to form the left-hand edge of the prisoner panel. No argument can be made for this alternative positioning, any more than it can be for the way Maler placed it, on the score of evident mating surfaces; but in Maler's photograph the design, which is none too clear in any case, does not seem to accord well with the expected hair or headdress of the prisoner. In our drawing one fragment may thus be represented twice; in the photograph the fragment has been left where Maler put it.

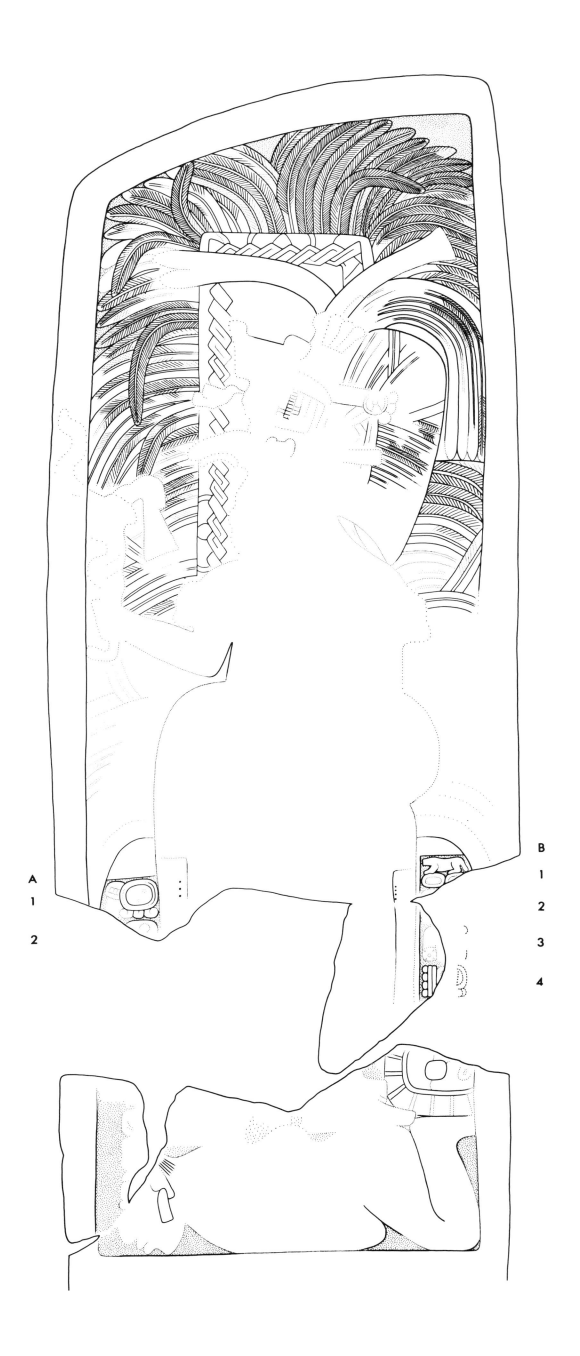

Xunantunich, Stela 8

LOCATION   The upper half was found by Schmidt lying on the south side of Structure A-6, parallel to the foot of the mound and a short distance to the west of Stela 1. The lower half, excavated by Palacio, lay farther to the west and likewise close to the foot of the substructure, with Stela 9 and a rectangular altar lying between the two halves. These now lie reunited under a protective roof in the plaza.

CONDITION   Broken in two, the upper half being quite well preserved, the lower much more eroded.

MATERIAL   Limestone.

SHAPE   Nearly parallel sides, with a narrow, flat top and sloping "shoulders."

DIMENSIONS
HLC   2.84 m
PB   1.62 m
MW   1.27 m
WBC   1.13 m
MTh   0.26 m
Rel   1.1 cm

CARVED AREAS   Front only.

PHOTOGRAPH   Graham, 1976.

DRAWING   Graham, based on a field drawing of the lower two-thirds only of the stela, corrected by artificial light.

A
1

2

3

B
1

2

C   D   E   F

Xunantunich, Stela 9

LOCATION   Found by Palacio on the south side of Structure A-6. It lay close to the foot of the substructure and parallel to it, between the lower part of Stela 8 and an uncarved rectangular altar. The stela has been moved a short distance and is housed under a roof.

CONDITION   Unbroken except for the two upper corners. The surface shows considerable erosion.

MATERIAL   Limestone.

SHAPE   Parallel sides, with unsymmetrically peaked top.

DIMENSIONS

HLC	2.20 m
PB	0.76 m
MW	1.28 m
WBC	1.28 m
MTh	0.33 m
Rel	1.0 cm

PHOTOGRAPH   Graham, 1976.

DRAWING   von Euw, based on a field drawing corrected by artificial light.

Xunantunich, Altar 1

LOCATION   Found apparently in front of the butt of Stela 1. In 1924 Gann, having had the hieroglyphic inscription and borders cut away, sent the figure of the skeleton, now lacking its right foot, to the British Museum. In 1938 Thompson, looking for the discarded glyph panel, found the site of the dismemberment, but the piece he sought had disappeared (Thompson field notes, Peabody Museum Archives, CIW 213, p. 21).

CONDITION   The upper left and lower right corners were broken off before discovery and have not been found. The degree of erosion is moderate.

MATERIAL   A dense limestone.

SHAPE   Almost square; Maler's photograph is distorted, not having been taken perpendicularly.

DIMENSIONS
Ht	0.75 m
MW	0.70 m
MTh	0.22 m
Rel	ca. 1.0 cm

PHOTOGRAPH   Reproduced from Maler's original negative of 1905.

DRAWING   Graham, based on a rectified print of Maler's photograph and a drawing of the surviving fragment in the British Museum.

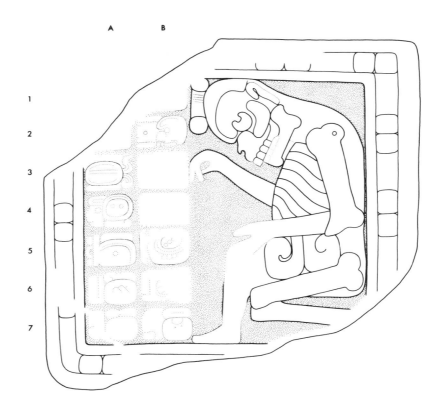